Don't Be a CopyCat!

Write a Great Report Without Plagiarizing

I promise not to plagiarize.
I promise not to plagiarize.
I promise not to plagiarize.
I promise not to

Nancy Bentley

 Enslow Publishers, Inc.
40 Industrial Road
Box 398
Berkeley Heights, NJ 07922
USA

http://www.enslow.com

Dedication: Eric and Peter, Sean and Cody, Nathan and Riley
Acknowledgements: My appreciation to the following professionals for their time, energy, and inspiration: Debbie Hickey, Karen Waters, Mike Herr, Doug Burwell, Gwen Giddons, Melissa Smead, and Barb Linnenbrink.

Enslow Elementary, an imprint of Enslow Publishers, Inc.

Enslow Elementary® is a registered trademark of Enslow Publishers, Inc.

Book Production: The Creative Spark; Wendy Mead, Editorial; Sandra Francis, Photo Research; Rob Court, Design and Illustrations.

Library of Congress Cataloging-in-Publication Data
Bentley, Nancy.
  Don't be a copycat! : write a great report without plagiarizing /
Nancy Bentley.
     p. cm.
  Summary: "A reference book for students in grades 3 and up on writing reports and avoiding plagiarism"—Provided by publisher.
  Includes bibliographical references and index.
  ISBN-13: 978-0-7660-2860-9
  ISBN-10: 0-7660-2860-7
  1. Report writing—Juvenile literature. 2. Plagiarism—Juvenile literature. I. Title.
  LB1047.3B46 2008
  371.3'0281—dc22
                                        2007024433

Printed in the United States of America

10 9 8 7 6 5 4 3 2

To Our Readers:
We have done our best to make sure that all Internet Addresses in this book were active and appropriate when we went to press. However, the author and publisher have no control over and assume no liability for the material available on those Internet sites or on other Web sites they may link to. Any comments or suggestions can be sent by e-mail to comments@enslow.com or to the address on the back cover.

Cover and Interior Illustrations: Rob Court

Interior Photos: Acclaim Images/Mitch Diamond, p. 46; Acclaim Images/Peter Casolino, p. 50; Associated Press/Mel Evans, p. 5; Associated Press/Kathy Willens, p.6; Associated Press/AP Photo, p. 9; Associated Press/NOAA, p. 15; Associated Press/Jae C. Hong, p. 30; Associated Press/Don Ryan, p. 53; Associated Press/Independent-Mail, Ken Ruinard, p. 56; The Image Works/Bob Daemmrich, p. 18; The Image Works/Ellen B. Senisi, p. 32; INMAGINE/Digitalvision, p. 3.

Contents

Chapter 1

In Your Own Words

It's time to write a report. Maybe your teacher gave you an assignment. Maybe you have a question of your own. You begin searching for information. You look in books. You use the Internet. You find answers, take notes, and start writing. Is that all there is to doing a report? No. You need to put the information together in the best way possible. And you must use the information without plagiarizing.

Plagiarism: What's That?

Plagiarism is taking someone else's work and pretending it's your own. "But I didn't steal anything," you say. "All I did was copy! How can it be wrong to copy something from a book or from the Web?"

Plagiarism happens when you take people's creative work without giving them credit. It could be their words, their music, or their photos. If you

It's important to listen carefully when a teacher gives out an assignment.

use other people's work and pretend it's yours, it's like robbing them.

This book will show you how to plan a report and take notes. It will explain how to use quotations, paraphrases, and summaries. It will give you suggestions for how to credit others' work properly. It also will show you how to ask for permission to use other people's work fairly. Best of all, this book will help you avoid plagiarism. All these things will make your own original work better.

A great report starts with good notes.

Original Work

Why is it so important to do original work? Your writing, painting, or composition is an expression of who you are. Only you could have created it. You are unique. Your hair

The word *plagiarism* comes from the Latin word *plagiarius,* meaning "kidnapper."[1]

color is probably different from your sister's. Your favorite food is different from your brother's. To unfairly use someone else's work and pretend it is your own is like pretending you are someone else. It is dishonest and unfair.

If you plagiarize, there will be consequences. At the very least, you'll feel embarrassed. Your teacher might give you a lower grade or ask you to write your report over. You may lose privileges at home and at school. Worst of all, those around you will no longer trust you. You will have to work hard to earn back their trust and respect. Plagiarism is a serious matter.

Who you are shapes what you create and how you express it. Laws protect that expression. Those laws are called copyright laws.

Chapter 2

Why Copyright Matters

Copyright protects original work. It protects stories, music, and art. But copyright did not always exist. In the old days, people told stories aloud. They didn't write them down. No one knew the name of the person who made up the story. It didn't matter. There was no copyright.

In the Middle Ages, it took years to make a book. Monks living in monasteries slowly copied books by hand. Books were rare and expensive. Then, in the mid-1400s, Johannes Gutenberg invented a movable-type printing press.[1] Movable type allowed a printer to arrange letters into sentences for each page. Gutenberg came up with a new way of putting blocks of type together. He used oil-based ink and a mechanical press. These changes made printing faster and less expensive. Several pages could be printed at the same time.

Books were printed in weeks, not years. More people began buying them. And booksellers began making more money.

Queen Anne ruled Great Britain from 1702 to 1714. During her reign, the first copyright law was created.[2] Before this, authors had little control over their work. Printers paid authors poorly. Fake copies were often printed and sold without the author's permission. The Statute of Queen Anne changed this. Writers became the owner of their printing rights for a limited amount of time. They could now profit from their work.

The framers of the U.S. Constitution liked the idea of copyrights. They soon created their own laws to protect original works.

At the Gutenberg Museum, a man dressed in traditional clothing shows how this early printing press works.

What Is not Protected by Copyright?

Not everything is covered by copyright. Here are some things that no one can copyright:[3]

1. Ideas—No one can copyright an idea. Copyright only protects the way you use words to express or tell an idea.

2. Common facts—Bats are mammals. That is a common fact, which cannot be copyrighted. When you take notes, you can copy down facts about bats. But you have to write them in your own words. If you copy those facts word for word from a book, you are copying an author's expression of those facts. You cannot state the information in the exact way the author wrote it without giving credit. That would be plagiarizing.

3. Names, lists of ingredients, alphabetical lists, titles, short phrases, slogans, and familiar symbols, such as a stop sign.

4. Phone books, calendars, lists of common facts, and titles of books.

5. U.S. government works, such as reports and statutes. (Statutes are laws passed by the legislature.)

6. Works in the public domain—The word *domain* can mean a place owned by a person or the

government. And everyone can be considered a member of the *public. Public domain* refers to works that can be used by anyone for free. When does a book become public domain? It might be so old that it was written before there were copyright laws. Or its copyright protection might have expired, or run out. Today, something written by an author can be copyright protected for the lifetime of the author, plus 70 years. After that, it moves into the public domain.

A *notice of copyright* shows that a work is copyright protected. The notice includes the © symbol, the date, and the creator's name.[4] A sample copyright notice would read "© 2009 Callie Androtti."

Understanding Fair Use

Copyright laws protect the rights of creators. In the 1990s, some people said these laws were too strict. They wanted to be able to use works more freely. But authors and producers objected. They were worried about people copying anything they wanted. They thought their work and income would be hurt by changes to the laws.

To fix this problem, the Conference on Fair Use met in 1997. Fair use gives certain people greater use of information without asking for

Know Your Terms

Copyright is a law that protects original works in eight categories: literary works, musical works, dramatic works, pantomimes and choreographic works, pictorial/graphic and sculptural works, motion pictures and other audiovisual works, sound recordings, and architectural works.

Don't Steal Other People's Stuff!

Plagiarism is pretending you created an original work when you didn't. It doesn't matter if what you copy is not protected by copyright. The amount you copy doesn't matter either. Whether you only use a small part of a book or the whole thing, it's still plagiarism. Any time you copy something and pretend that you created it, you have plagiarized.

permission. To see if you qualify for fair use, answer the following questions:

1. **What is your purpose?** Schools are nonprofit organizations. The purpose of nonprofit groups is to support the public good, not to make money. Schools may copy materials to support

student research and learning. However, teachers and students must still follow the fair use guidelines to see how much they may copy. (See page 48 in Chapter 6.)

2. **What is the nature of the work?** Ask yourself what type of work you want to copy. Is it fiction or nonfiction? With nonfiction works, you need to know that facts by themselves cannot be protected. So you can use some of the information given, but you cannot take it word for word from the book. In fiction and nonfiction, the way writers put down their words, or express themselves, is carefully protected.

3. **How much of the work is used?** The more you use, the less you may be protected by fair use. For example, you can't copy four paragraphs from an eight-paragraph story. That's just not playing fair.

4. **What is the effect on the market (the sales of the work)?** Will your use of the information make people not want to buy the original? If you copy something and then try to make money from it, that is not a fair use. This would harm the original creator.

Chapter 3

The Research Process

The research process is a series of steps that help you create good reports. Let's take a look at how it can help you avoid plagiarism.

 Step 1: Start with a topic, idea, or question
Step 2: Locate resources
Step 3: Take notes and examine the facts
Step 4: Write your report
Step 5: Evaluate your work

Step 1: Start with a topic, idea, or question
Research begins with a good topic, idea, or question. Don't worry if everyone in your class has the same topic. Use a different point of view or an unusual question. This will make your report stand out.

Let's say your class is studying weather. What interests you? Are you curious about clouds?

This image of Earth taken from space could be a good source for a report on clouds or storms.

Do you like to watch weather reports on hurricanes? If you get excited about a subject, you know that you are on the right track. It's also good to check in with your teacher to make sure your final topic is right for the assignment.

Read as much as you can about a topic before you begin to write. It is much easier to write a report in your own words if you understand the topic well. Plagiarism happens when you know too little. Then you are tempted to copy too much.

What's the Big Idea?

To begin your report, look at the scope of your topic. If your topic is too broad, you'll be swamped with too many facts. But if your topic is too narrow, you may not find enough.

A KWL chart[1] can help you make sure your topic is just the right size. It will help you sort your ideas. It includes the things you already know (K), the things you want to know (W), and the things you learned (L) after working on your report.

The "What I Know" column is for what you already know about your topic. Write down as many facts as you can. If you can't think of anything for this part, do more reading or change your topic.

Next, fill in the "What I Want to Know" column by coming up with as many questions about your topic as you can. This will help you decide what your report should focus on. Have fun with it. This is your chance to find an interesting point of view.

The last column is for you to work on later. Fill in the "What I Learned" column after you've completed your research.

KWL Chart **Topic:** Clouds		
What I **K**now	What I **W**ant to Know	What I **L**earned
• It rains when there are clouds in the sky. • Sometimes clouds don't cause rain.	• The names of different kinds of clouds. • How clouds are made. • How clouds affect weather. • Why clouds are different colors.	• There are cirrus, cumulus, stratus, and altostratus clouds. • Clouds are formed by rising water vapor. • If you know the types of clouds in the sky, you can predict weather. • The color of clouds depends on how thick they are and how much light shines through them.

What's Your Question?

You need questions to guide your research. Not all kinds of questions are the same. Some can be answered with one word. Others take much longer to answer. For a report, you want a question that fits the size of your assignment. Think about building a clubhouse. Before you start, you have to ask yourself how wide it should be. Then you need to ask how tall you want it to be. A good researcher asks similar questions. Let's look at three levels of questions.

Once you come up with your questions, a librarian can help you find good sources to use.

Laying Your *Foundation*

Basic questions can be answered with simple facts. Here are some examples for a report on clouds:

- How many types of clouds are there?
- What is the name for scientists who study clouds?
- How do scientists measure moisture in clouds?

Building Your *Walls*

It's time for more questions. Using your foundation, you will need to add walls, nails, and paint. This means you want to find questions that build on the simple facts. These could be questions that compare and contrast different facts. They could be questions that apply those facts to the real world. Here are a few examples for the report on clouds:

- Why are clouds important?
- How are cirrus clouds similar to or different from stratus clouds?
- Has Earth always had the same kinds of clouds?
- How do ordinary clouds turn into tornadoes?

Putting on Your *Roof*

You have built a foundation. The walls are up. Now it's time for a roof. Rooftop questions challenge you to think big. Ask questions about how your topic affects you, your town, and even your planet.

Examples would be:
- What would happen if we didn't have clouds?
- Should people try to make rain?
- When it isn't raining enough, how can my school cut down on its use of water?

Now you have your questions. You can make a graphic organizer, a "picture" that can help you see how those questions are connected to your topic. This can also help you see how they are related to each other.

Sample "House" Graphic Organizer

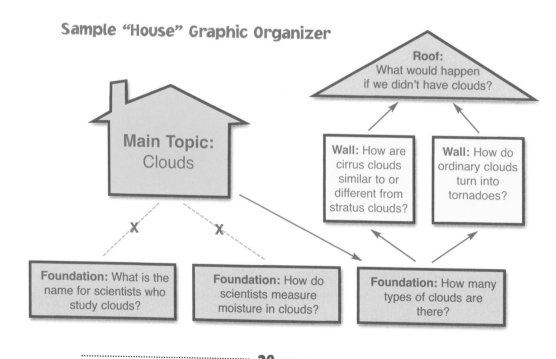

Chapter 4

Know Your Sources

Information is everywhere. You can find it in books, on the Web, at school, or at home.

Step 1: Start with a topic, idea, or question

Step 2: Locate resources

Step 3: Take notes and examine the facts

Step 4: Write your report

Step 5: Evaluate your work

Step 2: Locate resources

It helps to know where to look for information. If you want an ice cream cone, where would you go? A hardware store or an ice cream parlor? Where to go for information depends on what you're looking for. Let's examine different kinds of resources.

Primary and Secondary Sources

Your teacher may have talked to you about primary and secondary sources. Here are some easy ways to tell them apart.

Primary source information comes directly from a person. A quick way for you to remember this is *Primary = Personal.* Primary sources include interviews, e-mails, letters, diaries, and speeches. They also include essays, videos, personal or government papers, patents, and songs.

Secondary sources are collections or summaries of primary source information. To remember the meaning of the term, think *Secondary = Summary.* Secondary sources include reference books, magazines, newspapers, and some nonfiction books. Not all nonfiction books are secondary sources. Biographies and books about history include both primary and secondary information. Electronic databases, most Web sites, brochures, and manuals are also secondary sources.

A speech given by the girl who just won a race is a primary source. The newspaper article that tells who won the race and gives a summary of the victory speech is a secondary source. If you have access to a primary source, try to use it!

Reference Materials

Reference sources put large amounts of information into a single book or set of books. You can find them on library bookshelves or on the Internet. Reference sources are secondary sources.

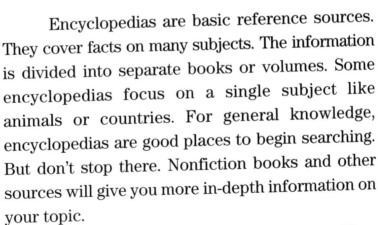

Use primary sources as much as you can. It will make your report much more interesting and accurate. How did President Abraham Lincoln feel during the Civil War? Read his letters. Read his words. This is a primary source. Don't just depend on second-hand information.

Encyclopedias are basic reference sources. They cover facts on many subjects. The information is divided into separate books or volumes. Some encyclopedias focus on a single subject like animals or countries. For general knowledge, encyclopedias are good places to begin searching. But don't stop there. Nonfiction books and other sources will give you more in-depth information on your topic.

Dictionaries tell you what words mean. They also tell you how to spell and pronounce words. If you need to know how to use a word correctly, look it up in a dictionary.

Almanacs are published every year. They are packed full of facts. Topics range from countries of the world to sports records. If you need to know the name of the longest river in the world, or who won the World Series three years ago, go to an almanac.

No matter where you find your information, be sure to credit your source. Include the author's name, book title, publisher, copyright date, and the page number.

Nonfiction Books

Nonfiction books cover a range of topics. They often go into more detail on a single topic than reference books. A nonfiction book about science or weather would be a good source for a report on clouds. Biographies and books about history often include primary sources such as parts of diaries or letters.

To find a good nonfiction book, evaluate it carefully. Check the copyright date to see if it is up to date. Who wrote the book? Is the author an expert on the subject? Does the author use facts to support his or her ideas? Is the reading level easy for you to understand? Is it written in a clear and well-organized manner? Does it have an index and table of contents? Does it have a bibliography that refers you to other sources?

Online Sources

The Internet can be a very good source for current information. If an earthquake strikes, the Internet will have the news before a newspaper or the TV news. But this speed can cause a problem. Online information is not always true. People in a rush to report a story might not have all the facts correct.

Anyone can put information on the Internet. That means some sites have mistakes in them. Check out the Web address. Who wrote the information? Find out how much that person knows about the topic. You want facts, not opinions or incorrect information.

What's a Good Web Site?

The Oregon School Library Information System has a few tips on how to find a good Web site:[1]

- You can easily find out who wrote or supports the site.
- There is an e-mail address or postal address for the author.
- The site loads easily, works the way it's supposed to, and has links that are all active.
- The information is easy to read.
- The site is interesting to look at and fun to spend time on.
- There is a date that shows when the site was made or updated.

Web sites like Yahoo! Kids, KidsClick!, and the WWW Virtual Library are called subject directories.[2] People make lists of sites organized by subject on these directories. This usually means there are fewer sites listed. But the ones that are listed are good sites that will fit your subject.

Other Web sites, like Google, are called search engines.[3] To use these, you type in keywords.

Searching Online

Should you begin your search with a broad topic or a narrow term? That depends!

For a broad search = use a subject search

If you have a broad topic in mind, begin with a subject search. This will help you find a lot of information. You can gather lots of facts. But be careful not to get overwhelmed with too much information. You will need to narrow your information to write a good report.

Example: *Subject = weather*

For a narrow search = use a keyword search

When you use an exact term or word, it is called a keyword search. This works well to find specific information. However, a keyword search can sometimes be too narrow. You may not find enough information for a whole report.

Example: *Keyword = thundercloud*

The search engine will give you a list of sites that use those words. You can sometimes end up with a lot of sites to look at. Use search engines when you are looking for exact sites or narrow topics.

Electronic databases are large collections of information.[4] They contain online encyclopedias, almanacs, and dictionaries. They also include magazine articles and Web sites. Libraries provide access to many of these special sources.

Other Sources

E-mail can be an interesting resource if your teacher gives you permission. For example, you can e-mail questions to an expert. A meteorologist's answers would be helpful for a report on clouds. His answers would be a primary source. But don't e-mail just anyone. You want to look for an expert who knows a lot about your topic.

Zoos and museums often have Web sites. Parks have brochures. Don't forget to look at those free resources.

Lastly, use your own life. Interview people close to you. Family, friends, and neighbors all have stories to tell. Photos, diaries, recordings, and home videos are fun to look at. They can also be good resources. But make sure to ask for permission first. Your Aunt Sally might not want you to show people the time her wig fell off during Thanksgiving dinner!

Chapter 5

Taking Notes

Taking good notes requires one thing. You must understand what you read. Are you looking up more than five words per page in a dictionary? If so, find another source. Plagiarism happens most often when you do not understand what you read. You begin to copy word for word.

Stop yourself in the middle of a paragraph. Can you tell a friend what you have read? If you can, you are ready to take notes. You are ready to examine the facts. You are ready to avoid plagiarism. If you can't, ask for help from an adult or friend. Check out another source.

Step 1: Start with a topic, idea, or
        question
Step 2: Locate resources
**Step 3: Take notes and examine
        the facts**
Step 4: Write your report
Step 5: Evaluate your work

Step 3: Take notes and examine the facts

How do you know what is important to write down? First, skim the source. Check the table of contents for your subject. Then look for clues in the text. Writers usually put main ideas in the first and last sentences of each paragraph. Read these carefully. Look for boldfaced words or italicized type. See if there are special boxes called "sidebars" alongside the text. Writers like to put special facts there.

There are two parts to the note-taking process: how to take notes, and where to put them. First, let's look at how to take notes.

The "How" of note Taking— Watching Your P's, Q's, and S's

Think of note taking as climbing a ladder. The closer you are to the ground, the closer you are to the original text. If you copy the exact words, you are writing down a quotation (Q). In the middle of the ladder, you change some of the sentences. You paraphrase (P), or rewrite the text in your own words. At the top of the ladder, you restate the main ideas in your own words and shorten the text. You summarize (S), or state the key points in your own way. Let's take a closer look.

Quotations

A quotation is a word-for-word copy. When would you use a quotation in your report? Use a quotation to capture a writer's style or give his or her exact words. Maybe you want to quote an expert. That would add authority to your report. Also, you could quote two different people to compare and contrast their ideas.

Always credit the source, and put quotation marks around the words you quote. That way, no one can say you plagiarized someone else's work.

Always make sure to write down which sources you found your quotations in.

Examples:

- Use **double quotation marks** at the beginning and end of the words quoted.

  Dr. Rich said, "Penguin Pete dove into the water."

- Use **single quotation marks** around a quotation inside a quotation.

  Dr. Rich later exclaimed, "Penguin Pete said, 'Don't plagiarize!' before diving into the water."

- If you leave out words inside a quotation, use **ellipses**, or three periods (…), to show the empty space.

  "We promise to name all sources we used because it's the right thing to do."

  "We promise to name all sources… because it's the right thing to do."

- Use **brackets** to add information inside a quotation that does not come from the original source.

  "Let's check our citations to make sure we spelled the publisher's name correctly."

  "Let's check our citations [our source notes] to make sure we spelled the publisher's name correctly."

- Another use for **brackets** is to replace a word from the original text to make it easier to read.

  "When you write your citation, use the Modern Language Association guidelines."

  "When you write your citation, use the [MLA] guidelines."

Read your source material carefully before creating a paraphrase.

- Set off a **short quotation** with quotation marks. Put it in the same paragraph as your own writing.

  Penguin Pete overheard another penguin telling a researcher, "Here in Antarctica, we have lots of time to read while sunning ourselves." It was the first time a penguin had spoken directly to a human.

- Set off a **long quotation** (more than three or four lines). Put it in a separate paragraph and indent it on both sides. It does not need to have quotation marks around it. Your teacher will tell you whether to double- or single-space the quote. Credit the author of the quote by including their name before the quote. This is called "giving attribution."

> *A great deal of research has been done on penguins in Antarctica, but this is the first time someone discovered that the birds were writing about how to avoid plagiarism. According to Dr. Harold Rich, Director of Food Supplies at the Penguin Pen,*
>
> > *...The birds probably started writing when the icebergs, pushing southward, closed off their usual breeding area. With extra time on their hands, scores of penguins began to write, making every effort to do so without plagiarizing.[1]*

In addition to giving attribution for your quote, you will also have to provide a citation. A citation is a note that tells what source the quote is from. The small number 1 at the end of the quote above refers the reader to the correct citation in the paper's footnotes or endnotes. You will learn how to create those later in this chapter.

Paraphrase

You paraphrase when you put something in your own words. First, read the text. Then, change the wording. You cannot just change a word or two. That would be plagiarizing. Anything that is still exactly the same as the original source should be set off with quotation marks.

A citation includes the author, title, publisher, and copyright date. Page numbers will help readers find the exact information in the source.

Example: Bentley, Nancy. Don't Be a Copycat! Write a Great Report Without Plagiarizing. Enslow Publishing, Inc., 2007, p. 34.

To paraphrase, you must change two things. Change the vocabulary and the order of ideas. A paraphrase is often shorter than the original text.[1] Within your paraphrase, give an attribution for the source. Also include a citation note in your footnotes or endnotes.

Steps for paraphrasing:
1. Read the text until you understand it.
2. Change vocabulary and the order of ideas.
3. Cite your source.

Original Text	Incorrect Paraphrase	Correct Paraphrase
"Macaroni penguins, largest of the crested penguins, are identifiable by their distinctive yellow crest feathers."	Macaroni penguins, largest of the crested penguins, can be identified by their yellow crest feathers.	According to Dr. Ace Fishbinder, Macaroni penguins have unusual yellow feathers on their head. This makes them easy to recognize.[1]
	[Too close to the original. The sentence order is the same. No credit is given to the original author.]	[Note that the source is credited within the text, and also with a citation note.]

PLAGIARISM ALERT!
Facts are free to use, but you cannot use them in exactly the same way another writer did. Use your own words, and cite the source.

Summarize

A summary is a short overview written in your own words. It includes only the main ideas, not all the details. It is shorter than a paraphrase.[2]

Steps for writing a summary:
1. Read the text until you understand it.
2. Write down the main idea in your own words.
3. Cite your source.

Original Text	Incorrect Summary	Correct Summary
"Due to overfishing, oil spills, and a 1°F increase in ocean temperatures, the Macaroni penguin population has recently dwindled by 30 percent. Fishbinder, along with many other scientists, now considers them a threatened species."	Overfishing has made Macaroni penguins a threatened species. **[Too short. Did not cover all the main ideas. No credit is given to original author.]**	Dr. Ace Fishbinder believes that overfishing, oil spills, and ocean warming may have made Macaroni penguins a threatened species.[1]

When you take notes, you gather other people's ideas. Use them to support or contrast with your own ideas. This will help you reach your own conclusions.

The "Where" of Note Taking

Should you take notes on writing paper or note cards? Does your teacher have a special method he or she wants you to use? What about electronic note taking? There is no single "right way" to take notes. Practice using a few different ways. Then decide which works best for you. Let's look at a few possibilities.

Method 1: Note Cards

This is the most common way to take notes. A note card can hold a single fact, phrase, or quotation. The advantage of using note cards is that they can be moved around. This is especially true if you color-code your cards. You can put all your notes about penguin feathers on cards with blue dots. Then you can put all your notes about penguin eggs on cards with yellow dots. When it's time to write your report, the note cards can be easily organized into paragraphs.

Method 2: Two-Column Notes

Another place to take notes is on a sheet of paper with two columns. Take a piece of paper and draw a line down the middle. In the left-hand column, put your questions or subtopics. On the right-hand side, take notes on supporting details. You can use a separate sheet of paper for each question or subtopic.

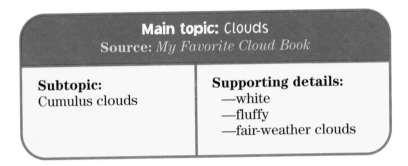

Main topic: Clouds
Source: *My Favorite Cloud Book*

| **Subtopic:** Cumulus clouds | **Supporting details:** —white —fluffy —fair-weather clouds |

Method 3: Graphic Organizers

You can also arrange your notes visually into graphic organizers. You did this earlier with your report questions on page 20 of Chapter 3. Another type of graphic organizer is a web. It extends out from the main point in the center, like a spider web.

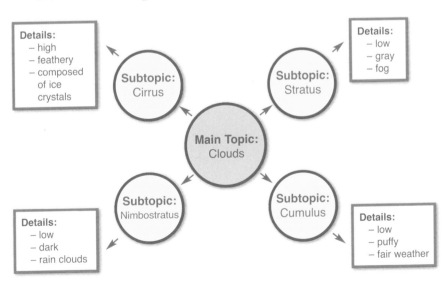

Method 4: Electronic Notes or E-notes

When you take notes from online sources, you can use your computer to take notes. Enter these electronic notes, or e-notes, into any word processing file. This is a way to help you remember what the original text was. Your teacher may have an e-note form to use, or you can make your own.

First, fill in the name of the Web site, the Web address, and the date. Web sites constantly delete, update, and change information. When you take notes, give your teacher the exact date you used the Web site. Cut and paste quotations or phrases into the Notes column. Then write a summary in your own words. E-notes help prevent plagiarizing by mistake. They help you track which words are yours and which words you borrowed. Remember to cite your source.

Sample E-note Form

Student: Lucas Jones	Date: November 16, 2008	Teacher/Class: Ms. Teller

Question/Topic: What kinds of clouds are there?

Web Site Title: Blustery Bob's University Weather One Site in My Home State
Web Address: http://www.myhomestate.univ.edu/weather

Notes:	Your summary:
Clouds are classified into groups based upon their height above the ground. They can be found at high, middle, or low ranges. Cirrus is an example of a high-level cloud group. Altostratus is a middle-level cloud group and stratus is an example of a low-level cloud group.	Blustery Bob, at the University Weather One Site, divides clouds into groups based on how high they are from the ground. Three common types are cirrus (high), altostratus (middle), and stratus (low).

When your report is finished, hand in your electronic notes. This will prove that you haven't plagiarized. Keep a copy for yourself.

Citations: As Easy as A, B, C, D, and Sometimes P

A citation includes the author, title, publisher, copyright date, and page number of each source. Every citation has the same basic parts. Ask your teacher which style he or she wants you to use. If your teacher does not have a favorite method, just remember to include these parts. It's as easy as A, B, C, D...and sometimes P! [3]

A = **A**uthor (or editor or publisher if no author)
B = Title of the **B**ook or work (underline the title of a book; put the title of an article in quotation marks)
C = Publishing **C**ompany or Web address
D = Copyright **D**ate or date you accessed the Web site
P = **P**age number (when appropriate)

Write your source at the top of each note card, graphic organizer, or page. Then, if you return your library book or your computer crashes, you can easily find your source again.

Understanding Notes

There are several ways to show your sources in your report. Check to see if the ways shown here will be okay for you to use. Your teacher may have another way that he or she would like you to use.

Footnotes or Endnotes

Footnotes or endnotes are probably the most common way of showing sources. Both use superscript numbers (small numbers placed higher than the regular words) in your report, just after the information you are giving credit for. The number refers the reader to the right footnote or endnote. That is where you will give the full citation for the source.

Footnotes are listed at the bottom (or foot) of the page. The numbers for footnotes go in order on each page, starting from 1 again on the next page. Endnotes are listed at the end of the report. The numbers for them go in order from the beginning of your report all the way to the end.

> This is what the superscript number looks like in your report:
>> According to Professor Samuel C. Lion, penguins go through a lot of fish.[2]

> This is what the footnote or endnote looks like:
>> 2. Lion, Samuel C. Penguins Afloat. Iceberg Press, 2007, p. 16.

Parenthetical Notes

Another way of showing your sources is to put the author's last name and the page number in parentheses in your report, just after the information you are crediting. Then you would put a list of works cited at the end of your report. That list would include all the sources you used in your report, in alphabetical order by the author's last name.

> This is what the parenthetical note looks like in your report:
>> According to Professor Samuel C. Lion, penguins go through a lot of fish. (Lion 16)

> This is how the source appears in your list of works cited:
>> Lion, Samuel C. Penguins Afloat. Iceberg Press, 2007.

In addition to your footnotes and endnotes, you should also give an alphabetical list of your sources at the end of your report. A bibliography includes all the sources you read for your topic. A list of works cited includes only the sources you actually used. This is necessary to include if you are using parenthetical notes instead of footnotes or endnotes.[4]

Here are some suggestions to help you remember the important parts of a citation:

Books
   A. Author (if more than one author, list both. Use the last name first.)
   B. Title (underlined)
   C. Publishing company
   D. Copyright date
   P. Page number(s)

Example:
   A. Fishbinder, Dr. Ace
   B. Macaroni Penguins
   C. Antarctica Books, Inc.
   D. 2004
   P. p. 15

Finished Citation:
   Fishbinder, Dr. Ace. Macaroni Penguins. Antarctica Books, Inc., 2004, p. 15.

Encyclopedias
   A. Author of article (editor or publisher if no author name is available)
   B. "Title of article" (use quotation marks) and Title of Encyclopedia Set (underlined)

C. Publishing company
D. Copyright date
P. Volume and page number(s)

Example:

A. Fishman, Ellen. (last name first)
B. "Macaroni Penguins" <u>The Junior World of Fish Encyclopedia</u>
C. World Fishing, Inc.
D. 2006
P. Vol. 10, pp. 157–160

Finished Citation:

Fishman, Ellen. "Macaroni Penguins." <u>The Junior World of Fish Encyclopedia</u>. World Fishing, Inc., 2006, Vol. 10, pp. 157–160.

Web Sites

A. Author (editor or publisher if no author)
B. "Title of article" (in quotation marks)
C. <Web site address (URL)> (in between the less-than "<" and greater-than ">" signs)
D. (Date Web site was visited) (in parentheses)

Example:

A. Weatherman, Stormy (last name first)
B. "Stormy Al's Weather Site"
C. <http://www.stormyalweathersite.com/clouds.htm>
D. (8/23/08)

Finished Citation:

Weatherman, Stormy. "Stormy Al's Weather Site." <http://www.stormyalweathersite.com/clouds.htm> (8/23/08).

E-mail
   A. Writer's name (last name first)
   B. "Subject line" (e-mail) (in quotation marks and parentheses)
   C. <Writer's e-mail address> (in between the less-than "<" and greater-than ">" signs)
   D. (Date of message) (in parentheses)

Example:
   A. Rainwater, Raymond
   B. "Cloud info" (e-mail)
   C. <rrainwater@myownplace.com>
   D. (7/5/08)

Finished Citation:
   Rainwater, Raymond. "Cloud info" (e-mail). <rrainwater@myownplace.com> (7/5/08).

Video
   A. Director and author
   B. Title and format (underline title)
   C. Company
   D. Date

Example:
   A. Carp, Marcella, director, and Trout, Brooke, writer
   B. Fish in the Sea (Videocassette)
   C. Beluga, Ltd.
   D. 2007

Finished Citation:
   Carp, Marcella, dir.; Trout, Brooke, writer. Fish in the Sea (Videocassette). Beluga, Ltd., 2007.

Chapter 6

Multimedia Matters

You may want to make your report stand out from the rest. You could make it a multimedia report. To do this, include pictures, sound, or movies with your text. Add a photo to your biography. Add a recording of "Yankee Doodle" to your history report. Add a hailstorm video to your science report. Make a slideshow with special software. Just do not turn into a "cut-and-paste plagiarizer." Remember to credit all your sources.

How can you make your report on the State of Michigan more interesting? Look for historic as well as recent photos. See if you can find the state song. Hunt for an old movie that shows a Model T car. These things will make your report come alive. As you do your research, make sure to look for pictures or sounds to go along with your text.

When you copy parts of an electronic file to your computer, it is called cutting and pasting. When you copy a whole file to your computer, it is called downloading. Practice good habits. Use e-notes to help yourself keep track of your sources. Print out Web pages so you can use their exact wording, or check to make sure you have paraphrased them correctly.

KNOW YOUR TERMS
Media refers to a form of communication like music, movies, or writing.
Multimedia is the combination of different kinds of media into a single work.

Many schools have music for student use. Some schools also have videos that students are allowed to use in school projects. Check with your school librarian.

Museums, zoos, and libraries have Web sites with special resources for teachers and kids. There are other Web sites with free resources. You can find free clip art and videos. These sites tell you if you can use their resources for free. If not, ask for permission. But either way, be sure to give them credit.

new Media

What about using podcasts or blogs? These can be good primary sources. You can hear a poet read

You can also create your own images to illustrate your report, such as taking photographs with a camera.

his poetry. You can quote from an interview with a scientist about her research. But first, ask your teacher for permission! And remember the risks. The information may not be accurate. The author may not be an expert. And it may take more time to search for useful information than with other sources.

KNOW YOUR TERMS

Podcasts are digital audio files. You can use a handheld device to hear them. Or you can use your computer. Video blogs are blogs with videos in them.

There are many places to find multimedia clips. But no matter which type of media you use, remember to:

- Give the name of the creator
- Cite the Web site address, the name of the page, and the date you found the information
- Add this to your list of sources at the end of your presentation
- Follow the fair use guidelines for the amount of material you use

Fair Use Guidelines

For school projects, there are a few rules to follow when using other people's work. The chart on the next page provides guidelines on how much you can use of different kinds of materials for your project. If you want to use more than what is given in these guidelines, ask permission from the creator.

PROTECT YOUR WORK!
When you finish your multimedia report, you may want to protect it. You have permission to show your work. But others do not. Put a note on your title slide telling others not to copy your work.[1]
Example: *Warning. Please do not copy.*

WARNING: Please Do Not Copy

Fair Use Guidelines for School Projects

Type of Media	Allowable Use[2]
Printed materials, such as books, magazines, or newspapers	You can quote up to 10 percent or 1,000 words of the source, whichever is less
Poetry	You can quote an entire poem of less than 250 words, but no more than 3 poems by one poet or 5 poems from one anthology (collection of poems)
Photographs and illustrations	Up to 5 images from any one artist or photographer
Music, lyrics, or music videos	Up to 10 percent of the source but no more than 30 seconds
Films and videos	Up to 10 percent of the source or 3 minutes, whichever is less

Chapter 7

The Writing Process

The facts are in. Your research is done. You found pictures, sound, and video. All your questions have been answered. Now, it's time to write your report!

> Step 1: Start with a topic, idea, or question
> Step 2: Locate resources
> Step 3: Take notes and examine the facts
> **Step 4: Write your report**
> Step 5: Evaluate your work

Outline First

First, organize your notes. Put them in order by main topics, key questions, or time. Then, begin writing. Your first sentence will tell the reader what that paragraph is about. Try to start each paragraph with a strong leading topic sentence. Think of it as "bait" to interest your readers. It should "hook" them with the paragraph's main idea. Add facts and supporting details to the rest of the paragraph. At the end of the paragraph, write a good transition to a new paragraph and the next topic in your report.

Main Topics

One way to outline is to use note cards. Put one fact on each card. Then cluster your facts around a topic. Organize your topics and fact cards into

Organize your ideas for your report by creating an outline.

paragraphs. Here is the beginning of an outline for a social studies report on Colorado:

I. **State of Colorado**
   A. Geography
      1. Rocky Mountains
         a. western part of state
      2. Prairie
         a. eastern part of state
   B. Native American tribes
      1. Ute Indians
         a. Northern Utes
         b. Southern Utes
      2. Pueblo Indians

Key Questions

Try outlining with key questions. This works well for science reports. For instance, here are sample questions for a report on clouds. What types of clouds are there? Are clouds always white? How do clouds affect our climate? Build individual paragraphs around these questions.

I. **Clouds**
   A. What types of clouds are there?
      1. Cirrus
      2. Altostratus
      3. Stratus
      4. Cumulus

B. What causes clouds?

    1. Rising water vapor

    2. Cool air

    3. Condensation

Time

If you want to write a biography, use dates in your outline. Start with the person's date of birth. Add important events. For the author J. K. Rowling, your outline might look like this:

I. J. K. Rowling, Writer

  A. Early Life

    1. Born July 31, 1965

    2. Grew up near Bristol, England

  B. Before she became a published author

    1. Taught in Scotland and Portugal in early 1990s

    2. Returned to England

    3. Finished writing first Harry Potter manuscript

  C. Writing career begins

    1. First book, <u>Harry Potter and the Philosopher's Stone</u>, published in England in 1997. (Title was later changed for the American version.)

Step 4: Write your report: The rough draft

It's time to write your report. Some people call the rough draft the "sloppy copy." Follow your outline.

Write the rough draft in your own words. Try to do it from memory. Think about what you found most interesting about the topic. This will help you avoid copying directly from your notes. Look at your notes only when you want to make sure you are on the right track.

Every report has a beginning, a middle, and an end. Put your main idea in the first paragraph. Start with a quotation, short anecdote (interesting story or event), or a fascinating fact. This will interest the reader in your subject. The middle of a paragraph or report is called the body. Include facts and details there. Compare and contrast information.

A teacher helps a group of students with their reports.

The end should be satisfying. Have the reader come away with more than basic facts. Try to make the reader care about the subject. Support your opinions with your findings. Build excitement right to the last sentence. End with your own personal insights. Tell the reader how this subject affects you. Tell readers how it will affect them, their community, and the world.

Step 1: Start with a topic, idea, or question
Step 2: Locate resources
Step 3: Take notes and examine the facts
Step 4: Write your report
Step 5: Evaluate your work

Step 5: Evaluate your work: The final draft

This is your final draft. It's time to check your writing. Look at your spelling and grammar. Did you vary the length of your sentences so they don't all sound the same? Did you use vivid verbs? Specific nouns? Colorful descriptions? Does the report sound like you and not like someone else?

You also want to make sure that all the information you used was correct. Did you present it in a clear way that is easy to follow? Did you cite your sources? And, last, double check your assignment. Did you include everything your teacher asked for? Cover page? Bibliography?

Congratulations on a job well done!

Chapter 8

Asking for Permission

When you use information, credit the source. *Always*. Even when you use the fair use guidelines. What happens if you want to use more information than the fair use guidelines allow? You will need to find the copyright owner. Once you find the owner, ask him or her for permission.

Asking for Permission

The person who owns a copyright is called the rights holder. He or she is the only one who can give you permission to use the work. But sometimes that person is no longer alive. His or her family or publisher may own the rights.

Let's say you want to copy a video. You found it on the Library of Congress Web site. Even though you found it there, the Library of Congress may not be able to give you permission to copy it.

It may not be the rights holder. This is true for all Web sites. Finding something on a Web site does not mean the Web site is the rights holder. The good news is that the owner of the Web site might help you find the rights holder.

Check with your parents and teacher before contacting someone to ask for permission. When you find the name and address of the rights holder, be patient. It may take weeks, even months to hear back from that person. If that's too long to wait, find another resource.

Web site managers put their e-mail addresses at the bottom of their home pages. Look for the word *contact*. You might need a mailing address. Ask a librarian to help you find one.

If you do an interview for your report, make sure to also ask the person for written permission to use it in your report.

DO NOT give anyone your e-mail or home address. Never. When you ask for permission, use your teacher's e-mail and your school's mailing address. But make sure to check that it's okay with your teacher first.

What Should You Include in Your Permission Request?

When you write your permission letter, make sure to include who, what, where, when, why, and how.

Who: Put your name on your request. With your teacher's permission, list your teacher's name and e-mail address, school phone and fax numbers, and grade level.

What: Tell the person exactly what you need. Be as specific as you can—how much of the document, image, video, or sound you want to use.

Where: Tell the person where you plan to put the material and how you plan to use it.

When: Tell the person the date you need the information and permission. Also give them the date your project is due. Make sure to give yourself enough time to add the materials after getting permission. You might also need time to change the report if you don't get permission.

Why: Describe your project. Tell the person the reason for your request.

How: Tell the person how many people will see it. Also explain what form people will see it in and whether you plan to make any money from it.

And remember—always thank the person for helping you!

Here are just a few examples of when you should ask for permission:

- If you want to send a friend's photo to others through e-mail
- If you want to use a whole song instead of just a few seconds of it
- If you want to make copies of your multimedia presentation to give to others
- If you want to use a picture from the Web for a fund-raising brochure, or for an item you want to sell

Your Work, Your Rights

Remember that you have rights, too. When you create something original, your work is protected. If someone wants to show your work outside the classroom, he or she must ask. Your parents or guardians can give permission on your behalf.[1]

So, create wonderful work. Put a copyright notice on it. Then go and celebrate. After all, you are an original, too!

Chapter Notes

Chapter 1 In Your Own Words

1. *Oxford English Dictionary*, 2nd edition. Oxford: Clarendon Press, 1989, p. 947.

Chapter 2 Why Copyright Matters

1. Arlene Bielefield and Lawrence Cheeseman, *Technology and Copyright Law: A Guidebook for the Library, Research, and Teaching Professions*, New York: Neal-Schuman Publishers, Inc., 1997, p. 6.

2. Bielefield, pp. 10–11.

3. Kenneth D. Crews, *Copyright Law for Librarians and Educators: Creative Strategies and Practical Solutions*, Chicago: ALA, 2006, pp.10.

4. Stephen Fishman, *The Copyright Handbook: How to Protect & Use Written Works*, Berkeley, CA: Nolo, 1999, 5th Ed., Ch. 2, p. 3.

Chapter 3 The Research Process

1. Donna Ogle, "K-W-L Plus: A Strategy for Comprehension and Summarization," *Journal of Reading*, 30, p. 626–63.

Chapter 4 Know Your Sources

1. "How to Evaluate Information," Oregon School Library Information System, 2006, <http://www.oslis.org/elementary/index.php?page=evaluateGood> (10/17/07).

2. Debbie Flannigan, "Subject Directories," 1999–2004, <http:// www.learnwebskills.com/search/subject.html> (10/17/07).

3. Debbie Flannigan, "Search Engines," 1999–2004, <http://www.learnwebskills.com/search/engines.html> (10/17/07).

4. "Introduction," n.d., <http://www.electronicdatabases.com/index.html> (10/17/07).

Chapter **5** Taking Notes

1. "Paraphrase: Write It in Your Own Words," *The Owl at Purdue*, 10/11/07, <http://owl.english.purdue.edu/owl/resource/619/01/> (10/17/07).

2. "Quoting, Paraphrasing, and Summarizing" *Owl Online Writing Lab*, Purdue University, 9/10/06, <http://owl.english.purdue.edu/owl/resource/563/01/> (10/17/07).

3. Mike Herr, "Citing Resources: Elementary," Steele Elementary School, 2007, <http://www.d11.org/steele> (11/14/07).

4. Holly Samuels, "Making a Works Cited," 2004, <http://www.crlsresearchguide.org/19_Making_Works_Cited.asp> (10/17/07).

Chapter **6** Multimedia Matters

1. Carol Simpson, *Copyright for Schools: A Practical Guide*, Worthington, OH: Linworth Publishing, Inc., 2005, p. 186.

2. Hall Davidson, "The Educator's Guide to Copyright and Fair Use," 2002, <http://www.techlearning.com/techlearning/pdf/db_area/archives/TL/2002/10/copyright_chart.pdf> (10/17/07).

Chapter **8** Asking for Permission

1. Carol Simpson, *Copyright for Schools: A Practical Guide*, Worthington, OH: Linworth Publishing, Inc., 2005, p. 190.

Glossary

blog—An online journal.

citation—A way to identify a book, film, magazine, or other source. A correct citation includes the name of the author, title, publisher, copyright date, and page used in the work.

cite—To provide the source of a piece of information or quotation.

copyright—Laws that protect original works. Many kinds of works are protected, including books, stories, plays, music, art, photographs, and films.

cut and paste—The electronic process of copying and moving sections of documents from one place to another.

downloading—Moving and saving text, photo, art, video, or audio files from the Internet to your computer.

electronic database—Large, computerized collection of information, statistics, and data. An electronic database may include articles from newspapers and magazines as well as encyclopedias and other reference books.

electronic notes—A form used for online note taking. Also called e-notes.

fair use—The term used to describe the reasonable use of copyrighted material.

keywords—Important words or short phrases related to a subject, which are used when trying to find more information on the topic.

multimedia—The combination of different kinds of media, such as text, graphics, audio, and video, to make a single work.

original work—A unique, new literary or artistic creation made by a writer or artist.

paraphrase—To rephrase a section of text in your own words.

permission—The process of asking to use someone's creative work.

plagiarism—The improper use of another person's creative work. This can include not giving credit or not asking for permission when using someone else's work.

podcast—A sound file that can be heard on a handheld device or a computer.

primary source—Information that comes directly from a person, such as a letter or a diary.

public domain—Creative works that either have no copyright or for which the copyright has expired. These works can be used by anyone without having to ask for permission, although credit should still be given to the original creator.

quotations—Word-for-word copies of text or speech.

rights holder—A person or organization who owns a copyright.

search engines—Computer programs that use keywords to search for information.

secondary sources—Material based on primary source materials; usually provide summaries of information found in the original sources.

statute—A kind of law created and approved by a government.

summary—A short overview of a section of text that only covers its main ideas.

URL—A Web site's address. The letters stand for Uniform Resource Locator.

Further Reading

Hamilton, John. *Primary and Secondary Sources.* Edina, MN: Abdo Publishing Co., 2005.

Janeczko, Paul B. *Writing Winning Reports and Essays.* New York: Scholastic Inc., 2003.

Jarnow, Jill. *Writing to Explain.* New York: PowerKids Press, 2006.

Ready, Set, Write!: A Student Writer's Handbook for School and Home. Time for Kids Books, 2006.

Internet Addresses

Copyright Kids Web site
http://www.copyrightkids.org

NoodleTools Web Site
http://www.noodletools.com/tools/freetools.php

Oregon School Library Information System
http://www.oslis.org/front-page

Index